How do you make a squid laugh?

With ten-tickles.

What do you get if you give a dinosaur a pogo stick?

Big holes in your driveway.

What is a volcano's favorite food?

Magma-roni and cheese.

Why did the fish cross the ocean?

To get to the other tide.

Poke your fingers through the holes to help the fish swim.

How do baby birds learn to fly?

They just wing it.

Why aren't grapes ever lonely?

They always come in bunches!

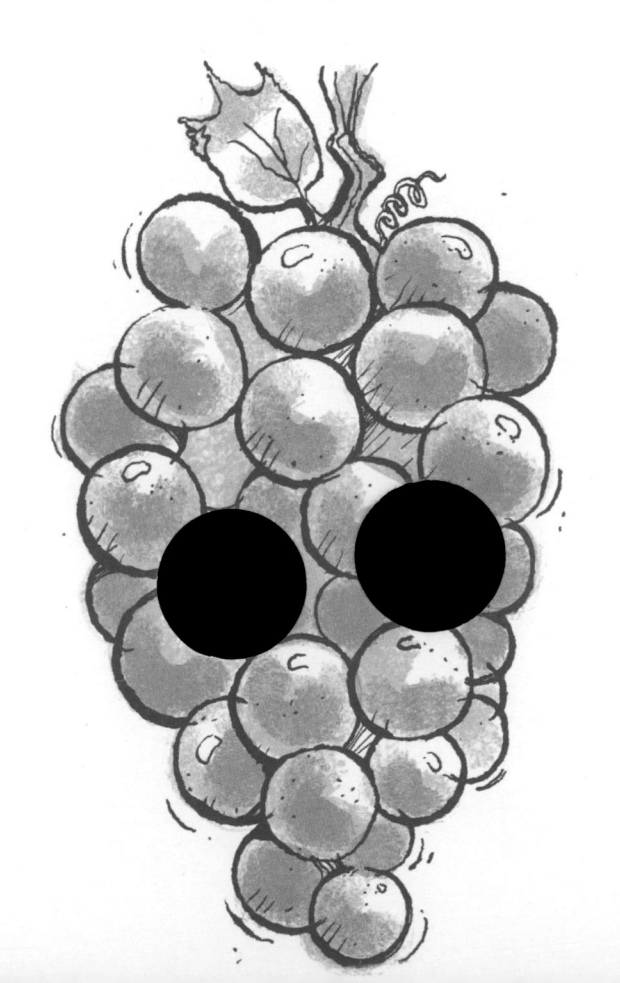

**What was purple
and conquered the world?**

Alexander the Grape.

Why do elephants have trunks?

They'd look pretty silly with glove compartments!

Poke your fingers through the holes to give the elephants trunks.

What did the cat say when he stubbed his toe?

"Me-ow!"

Knock, Knock.
Who's there?
Cargo.
Cargo who?
No, car go beep, beep.

Knock, Knock.
Who's there?
Police.
Police who?
Police stop telling knock-knock jokes.

What did the snake say to his little sister?

"Stop being such a rattle-tail!"

Poke your fingers through the holes to make their tails move.

What did the boy say when his dog ran away?

"Well, doggone!"

What do you call an alligator in a vest with binoculars?

An investigator.

What do you call the leader of the popcorn?

A kernal.

Knock, Knock.
Who's there?
Jester.
Jester who?
Jester minute, I'm trying to find my keys.

Poke your fingers through the holes to help the jester juggle.

Why did the boy eat his homework?

Because he didn't have a dog.

What does one comet say to another when they pass by each other?

"Glad to meteor!"

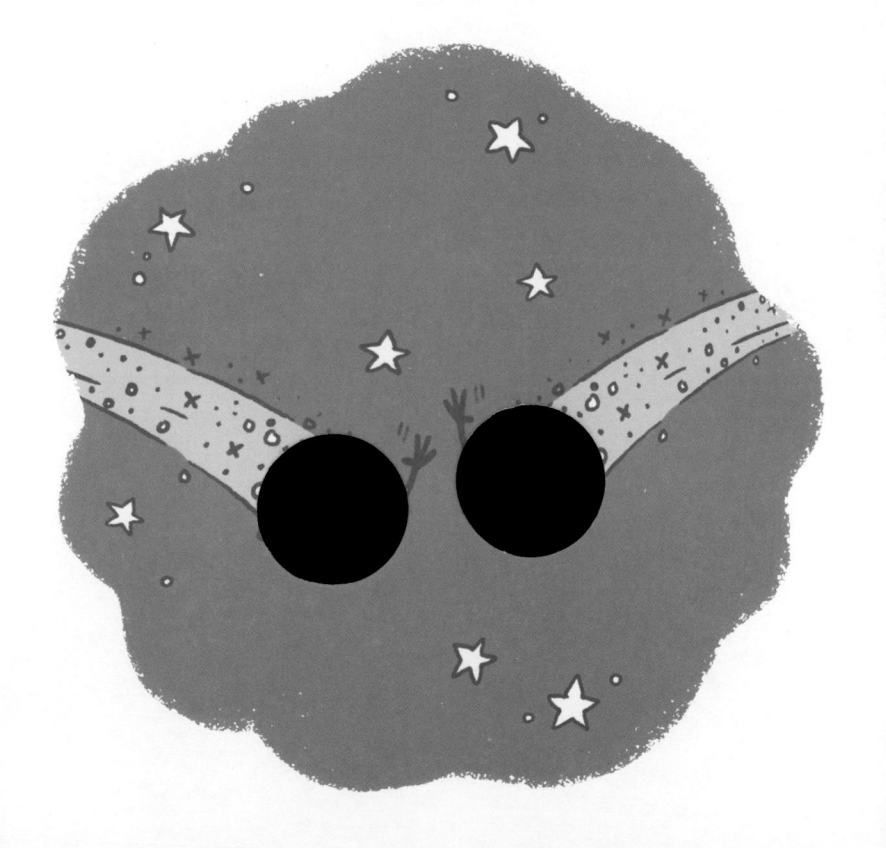

What did the 0 say to the 8?

"Hey, nice belt!"

What's worse than finding a worm in your apple?

Finding two worms in your apple.

Poke your fingers through the holes to add worms to the apple.

Knock, knock.
Who's there?
Cook.
Cook who?
Hey, who are you calling cuckoo?

Knock, knock.
Who's there?
Chick.
Chick who?
Chick out my new skateboard!

Why is it better to eat doughnuts in the rain?

You get more sprinkles.

What's the difference between a fish and a piano?

You can tune a piano, but you can't tuna fish.

Poke your fingers through the holes to make the fish play piano.

What is a balloon's least favorite music?

Pop!

Why are old socks good for golf?

Because they have plenty of holes!

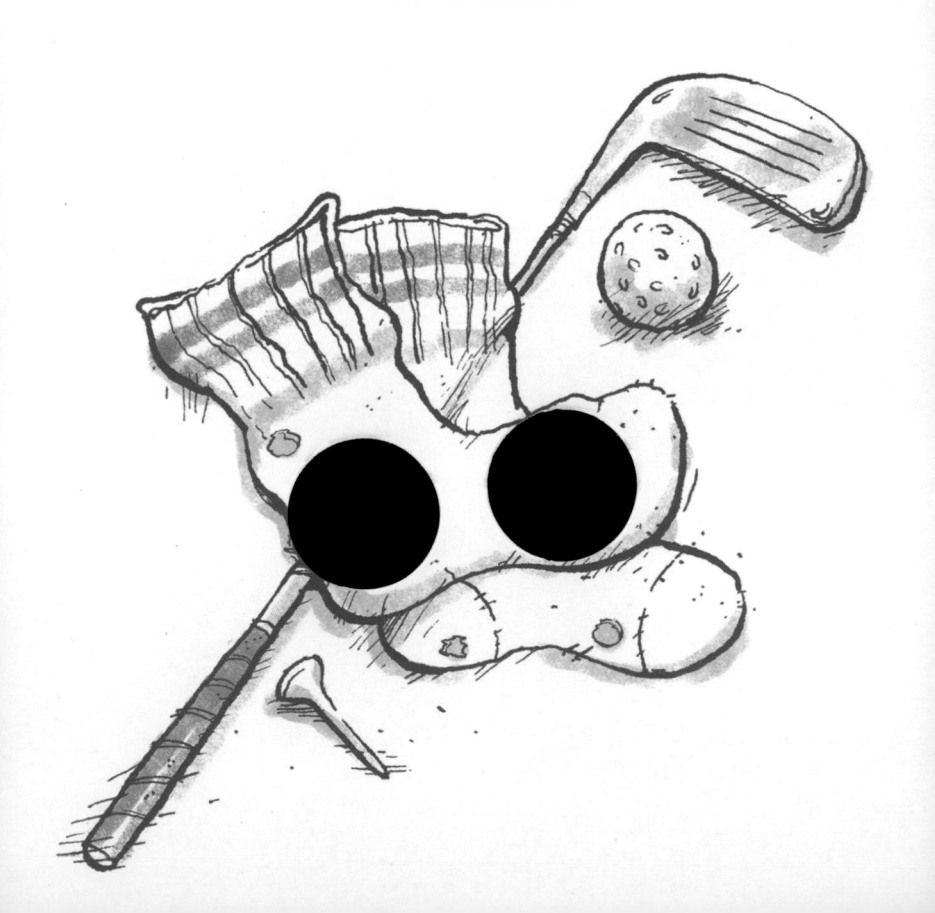

What letter is always surprised?

O.

How do spiders learn definitions?

They use Webster's Dictionary.

Poke your fingers through the holes to add more spider legs.

Why did the book go to the doctor?

Because it hurt its spine.

What kind of coat is always wet when you put it on?

A coat of paint.

What's a cow's favorite painting?

The Moona Lisa.

What did the turtle say to his friend when he left?

"Turtle-oo!"

Poke your fingers through the holes to make the turtles talk to one another.

Use a dry-erase marker to draw your own googly-eyed character below—then wipe it off and draw again!